Who Were the Barbarians?

Ancient Rome History for Kids
Children's Ancient History

The Roman Empire crumbled under pressure from migrating peoples and armies. The Romans called these peoples "the barbarians". Who were they, and why did they invade the Roman Empire? Read on to find out!

The Late Roman Empire

The Roman Empire had long been the most powerful political, cultural, and military force in Europe, the Middle East, and North Africa. Rome's legions, road-builders, legal and political structures, and civic leaders controlled and influenced a region that stretched from the border of Scotland to what is now Iran.

But by the fifth century Rome's leaders realized that the empire was too large, and faced too many enemies, for the government to control everything from Rome. The empire became two empires, the Western Roman Empire and, in the east, what became known as the Byzantine Empire. Read the Baby Professor Book The Byzantine Empire to learn more about the empire in the east.

On top of fighting external enemies ranging from the Parthian Empire in the east to Germanic tribes in the north, the two empires sometimes fought each other. This weakened the whole Roman structure. The Roman Empire, even just the western half, was trying to hold on to too much territory with not enough resources. Paying for an army to control such a large territory is expensive, and it was hard to raise enough in tax money to pay the bills.

The Barbarians

The word "barbarian" comes from a Greek phrase to describe foreigners who could not speak Greek well. It basically meant, "Those folks who say bla-bla-bla when they talk."

The Romans adopted the phrase to describe people who lived beyond the borders of the Empire and who did not have a culture the Romans recognized. The Parthians, to the east, were long-time and respected enemies. But the people to the north and east in Europe seemed to the Romans to be lesser, to have no culture, to be, in a word, barbaric.

Rhine River

For a long time the Romans kept a strong border mainly along the Rhine River, with the Empire south of the river and dark forests full of barbarians to the north. As the Empire needed more soldiers for the never-ending wars, Rome started letting Germanic tribes across the Rhine to settle in the Empire in exchange for military service.

But north and east of the Germanic tribes were other peoples—the Goths, the Vandals and others. In the fourth century tribes and peoples even further east toward China, particularly the Huns, started pushing west as Chinese and Mongol peoples pushed on them. This pressed the barbarian peoples to try to move west, and to fight with Rome when the Empire tried to resist them.

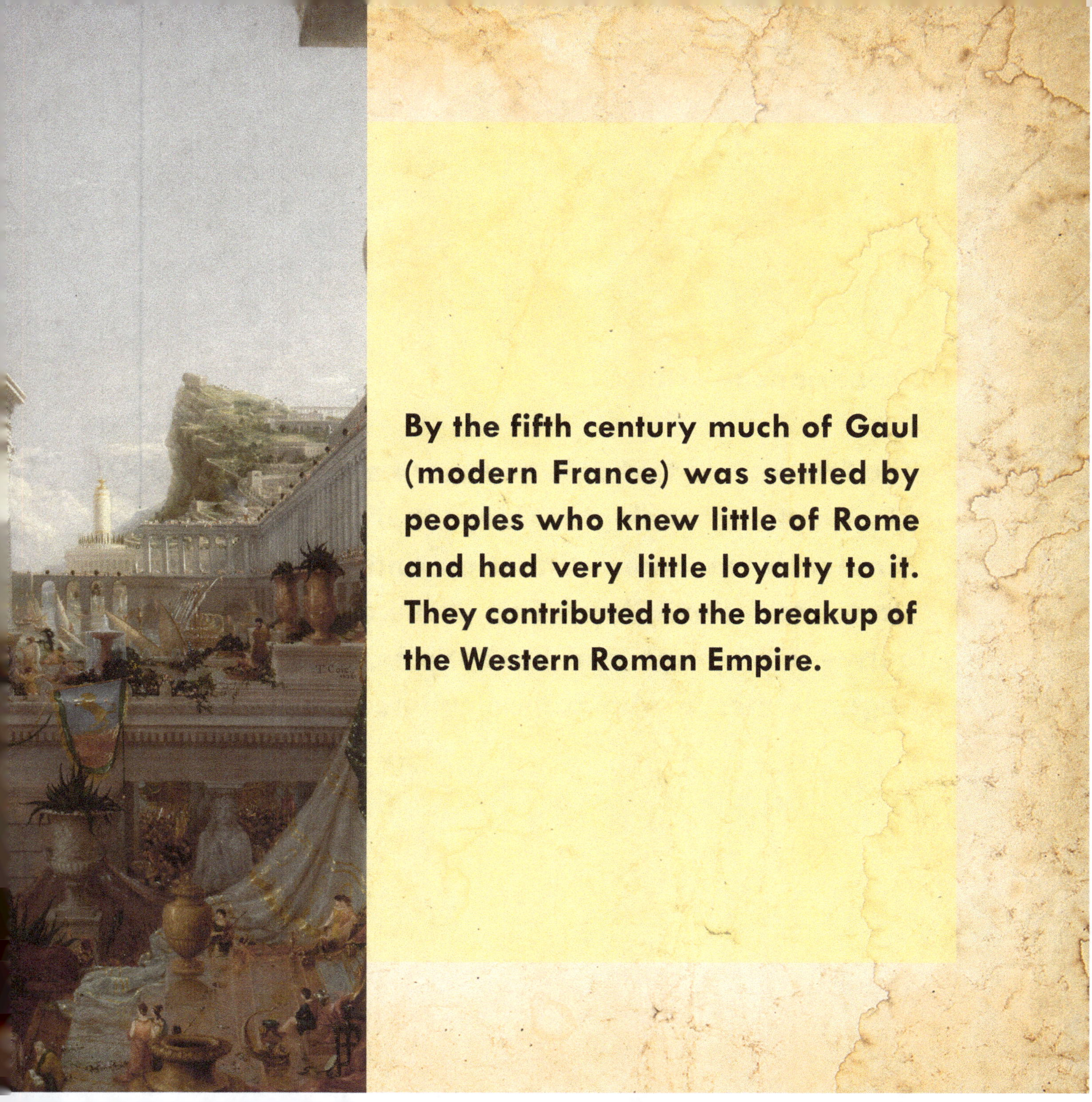

By the fifth century much of Gaul (modern France) was settled by peoples who knew little of Rome and had very little loyalty to it. They contributed to the breakup of the Western Roman Empire.

Barbarians in France

The Franks ruled what is now northern France by 500 CE. The first of their great kings that we know of was Clovis. He became a Christian and his people also started to follow Christ. This broke down one barrier between Romans and barbarians, and the Franks began to merge with Roman culture.

Clovis made the village of Paris his capital, and he extended his control toward the south. He died in 511, but Frankish kings after him slowly continued to expand Frankish rule. When Islamic armies from Spain, the Moors, invaded France, the Frankish king Charles Martel led the army that defeated them at Poitiers in 732. His son, Charlemagne (Charles the Great) became very powerful and claimed to be the new Emperor in Europe.

Barbarians in Spain

Around 400 two barbarian tribes, the Sueves and the Vandals, fought and pillaged their way right through France, crossed the Pyrenees Mountains, and conquered most of what is now Spain.

In 416 the Visigoths made a treaty with the Romans. They pursued the other tribes into Spain and won many victories. The Visigoths withdrew for a while and during that time the Vandals moved on to North Africa, leaving the Sueves in Spain. Only one little part of Spain was still under Roman control. Around 450 Theoderic II, king of the Visigoths, invaded Spain again. He destroyed the Sueve armies and most of Spain became Visigothic territory.

However, Visigothic Spain was never very powerful. When Islamic armies, the Moors, crossed from Morocco into Spain in the seventh and eighth centuries, they took over Spain quite quickly. An army of Berber tribesmen and Arabs wiped out the army of the Visigoths in a battle in 711.

Barbarians in North Africa

When the Vandals left Spain for North Africa, they conquered one Roman province after another, until all of North Africa was in their hands. They made their main city at Carthage, which had been Rome's rival even before Rome was an empire.

Rome depended heavily on the grain grown and shipped from North Africa. Without that supply, the collapse of the Roman Empire came even more quickly.

However, with the rise of Islam, Arab and tribal armies defeated the Vandals over and over again. Between 640 and 710, the Arab armies moved from east to west until the Vandal kingdoms of North Africa were all conquered.

Barbarians in England

The Saxons, from northern Germany, had been raiding parts of England since early in the third century. But as the Roman legions withdrew in the fourth and fifth centuries, Saxon and Viking tribes began making permanent settlements in England, Scotland, and Ireland. The last Roman forces left the island in 407.

The small native kingdoms that emerged in England as Rome withdrew tried to work out some sort of arrangement with the raiders. They invited the Jutes to take part of English territory in exchange for helping to defend England against other tribes. But the arrangement did not last. The Jutes, and then the Saxons, took more and more of southern England.

Something happened to slow the invasion around 500, and tradition says that is when King Arthur won victory after victory. We don't know for sure that there was a real King Arthur, and he may have been a general rather than a king, but at that time the barbarians lost ground throughout the island.

By 550 or so the original people of England, the Celts, were overrun by Jutes, Picts, Saxons, Angles (who gave their name to the island) and other invading tribes. Only Wales and the west of England held out longer.

In the seventh century England was a patchwork of small kingdoms. Gradually the people became Christian and the barbarian peoples mixed with the original peoples of the island. By then end of the seventh century most of England was Christian and often at peace.

Barbarians in Italy

In 410 the Goths, under Alaric, moved south from Germany through Gaul and into Italy. They defeated several already-weakened Roman armies and captured Rome itself.

The Goths did not hold Rome at that point, and the Roman Empire recovered and managed to continue for most of the next century. However, the Vandals, who now controlled North Africa, both cut off the grain supplies for Rome and launched raids into Italy. In 455 the Vandals captured Rome and sacked it—that means they took anything of value they could find, destroyed the defensive walls and many buildings, and killed or took as slaves many people. Finally, Odoacer, a German soldier, deposed the last Roman emperor in 476 and declared himself King of Italy. The Roman Empire in the West was no more.

This was not a total collapse, thought. Although the Roman military might was gone, its cities continued and people continued to plant and harvest crops. The Germanic kings adopted much of Roman culture, its laws, and its local political structures. As much as the barbarians conquered Rome, Rome converted the barbarians.

After Odoacer died in 493, Theodoric the Ostrogoth (another tribe!) became King of Italy. He was king and kept the area at peace until his death in 526.

6035. P. Z. - CONSTANTINOPLE - LA PLACE EMIN-ONOU ET YENI DJAMI

In the east, the Byzantine Empire was still strong. It was expanding its territory to the east and south, and in 535 Emperor Justinian sent an army to invade Italy. The emperors had not fully accepted that the original Roman Empire was too large to govern and control, and Justinian wanted to "restore" imperial control over all former Roman territory.

There was a long series of wars that ruined cities, destroyed crops, and killed many people. The Byzantine armies were victorious at first and captured Ravenna in 540, but then the Goths began to have more success. By 562 there was no Byzantine territory left in Italy, but the scars of war took a long time to heal.

In 568 another tribe, the Lombards, invaded north Italy. They won victory after victory against the Goth and Byzantine armies. Finally the Byzantine forces were able to stop Lombard expansion from going further south than Rome. From that time on the story is no longer about barbarians, but about Italians.

**Each Ending
is a Beginning**

**What happened in the past
helps shape our present
and future. Read other Baby
Professor books, like Daily
Life of a Roman Family in
the Ancient Times, to learn
more!**

Visit
BABY PROFESSOR
EDUCATION KIDS
www.BabyProfessorBooks.com
to download Free Baby Professor eBooks
and view our catalog of new and exciting
Children's Books